CATHOLIC SUNDAY AND DAILY MASS READINGS

For DECEMBER 2024

[Book 12 of 12]

Catholic Missal, Lectionary with Celebrations of the Liturgical Year 2024 [Year B]

Dear Reader,

Thank you for purchasing and reading this book.

I sincerely thank you for your trust. Let us pray together and invite our Lord in Heaven into everyday life.

If you like this book, please don't hesitate to tell your friends and family about it so that more people can benefit. Thank you again for your support, and happy reading.

May our Savior be glorified, and may He bless you. Amen.

CONTENTS

PART I

a. PRINCIPAL CELEBRATIONS OF THE LITURGICAL YEAR B, 2024

CELEBRATIONS	DATE
First Sunday of Advent, Year B	December 3, 2023
Ash Wednesday	February 14, 2024
Easter Sunday	March 31, 2024
The Ascension of the Lord (Sunday)	May 12, 2024
Pentecost Sunday	May 19, 2024
The Most Holy Body and Blood of Christ (Corpus Christi)	June 2, 2024
First Sunday of Advent, Year C	December 1, 2024

b. CYCLES - LECTIONARY FOR MASS

Sunday Cycle	Year B	December 3, 2023 to November 24, 2024
Weekday Cycle	Cycle II	January 9 to February 13, 2024 May 20 to November 30, 2024
Sunday Cycle	Year C	December 1, 2024 to November 23, 2025

PART II

SUNDAY AND DAILY MASS READINGS 2024

DECEMBER 2024

December 1, 2024

First Sunday of Advent

First Reading: Jeremiah 33: 14-16

14 Behold the days come, saith the Lord, that I will perform the good word that I have spoken to the house of Israel, and to the house of Juda. 15 In those days, and at that time, I will make the bud of justice to spring forth unto David, and he shall do judgment and justice in the earth. 16 In those days shall Juda be saved, and Jerusalem shall dwell securely: and this is the name that they shall call him, The Lord our just one.

Responsorial Psalm: Psalms 25: 4-5, 8-9, 10, 14

R. (1b) To you, O Lord, I lift my soul.

4 Let all them be confounded that act unjust things without cause. shew, O Lord, thy ways to me, and teach me thy paths.

5 Direct me in thy truth, and teach me; for thou art God my Saviour; and on thee have I waited all the day long.

R. To you, O Lord, I lift my soul.

8 The Lord is sweet and righteous: therefore he will give a law to sinners in the way.

9 He will guide the mild in judgment: he will teach the meek his ways.

R. To you, O Lord, I lift my soul.

10 All the ways of the Lord are mercy and truth, to them that seek after his covenant and his testimonies.

R. To you, O Lord, I lift my soul.

14 The Lord is a firmament to them that fear him: and his covenant shall be made manifest to them.

R. To you, O Lord, I lift my soul.

Second Reading: First Thessalonians 3: 12 – 4: 2

12 And may the Lord multiply you, and make you abound in charity towards one another, and towards all men: as we do also towards you,*13* To confirm your hearts without blame, in holiness, before God and our Father, at the coming of our Lord Jesus Christ, with all his saints. Amen.*4:1* For the rest therefore, brethren, we pray and beseech you in the Lord Jesus, that as you have received from us, how you ought to walk, and to please God, so also you would walk, that you may abound the more.*2* For you know what precepts I have given to you by the Lord Jesus.

Alleluia: Psalms 85: 8

R. Alleluia, alleluia.

8 Show us, Lord, your love; and grant us your salvation.

R. Alleluia, alleluia.

Gospel: Luke 21: 25-28, 34-36

25 And there shall be signs in the sun, and in the moon, and in the stars; and upon the earth distress of nations, by reason of the confusion of the roaring of the sea and of the waves;26 Men withering away for fear, and expectation of what shall come upon the whole world. For the powers of heaven shall be moved;27 And then they shall see the Son of man coming in a cloud, with great power and majesty.28 But when these things begin to come to pass, look up, and lift up your heads, because your redemption is at hand.

34 And take heed to yourselves, lest perhaps your hearts be overcharged with surfeiting and drunkenness, and the cares of this life, and that day come upon you suddenly.35 For as a snare shall it come upon all that sit upon the face of the whole earth.36 Watch ye, therefore, praying at all times, that you may be accounted worthy to escape all these things that are to come, and to stand before the Son of man.

December 2, 2024

Monday of the First Week of Advent

First Reading: Isaiah 2: 1-5

1 The word that Isaias the son of Amos saw, concerning Juda and Jerusalem.2 And in the last days the mountain of the house of the Lord shall be prepared on the top of mountains, and it shall be exalted above the hills, and all nations shall flow unto it.3 And many people shall go, and say: Come and let us go up to the mountain of the Lord, and to the house of the God of Jacob, and he will teach us his ways, and we will walk in his paths: for the law shall come forth from Sion, and the word of the Lord from Jerusalem.4 And he shall judge the Gentiles, and rebuke many people: and they shall turn their swords into ploughshares, and their spears into sickles: nation shall not lift up sword against nation, neither shall they be exercised any more to war.5 O house of Jacob, come ye, and let us walk in the light of the Lord.

Responsorial Psalm: Psalms 122: 1-2, 3-4b, 4cd-5, 6-7, 8-9

R. Let us go rejoicing to the house of the Lord.

1 I rejoiced at the things that were said to me: We shall go into the house of the Lord.

2 Our feet were standing in thy courts, O Jerusalem.

R. Let us go rejoicing to the house of the Lord.

3 Jerusalem, which is built as a city, which is compact together.

4ab For thither did the tribes go up, the tribes of the Lord.

R. Let us go rejoicing to the house of the Lord.

4cd The testimony of Israel, to praise the name of the Lord.

5 Because their seats have sat in judgment, seats upon the house of David.

R. Let us go rejoicing to the house of the Lord.

6 Pray ye for the things that are for the peace of Jerusalem: and abundance for them that love thee.

7 Let peace be in thy strength: and abundance in thy towers.

R. Let us go rejoicing to the house of the Lord.

8 For the sake of my brethren, and of my neighbours, I spoke peace of thee.

9 Because of the house of the Lord our God, I have sought good things for thee.

R. Let us go rejoicing to the house of the Lord.

Alleluia: Psalms 80: 4

R. Alleluia, alleluia.

4 Come and save us, LORD our God; let your face shine upon us, that we may be saved.

R. Alleluia, alleluia.

Gospel: Matthew 8: 5-11

5 And when he had entered into Capharnaum, there came to him a centurion, beseeching him,*6* And saying, Lord, my servant lieth at home sick of the palsy, and is grieviously tormented.*7* And Jesus saith to him: I will come and heal him.*8* And the centurion making answer, said: Lord, I am not worthy that thou shouldst enter under my roof: but only say the word, and my servant shall be healed.*9* For I also am a man subject to authority, having under me soldiers; and I say to this, Go, and he goeth, and to another, Come, and he cometh, and to my servant, Do this, and he doeth it.*10* And Jesus hearing this, marvelled; and said to them that followed him: Amen I say to you, I have not found so great faith in Israel.*11* And I say to you that many shall come from the east and the west, and shall sit down with Abraham, and Isaac, and Jacob in the kingdom of heaven:

December 3, 2024

Memorial of Saint Francis Xavier, Priest

First Reading: Isaiah 11: 1-10

1 And there shall come forth a rod out of the root of Jesse, and a flower shall rise up out of his root.2 And the spirit of the Lord shall rest upon him: the spirit of wisdom, and of understanding, the spirit of counsel, and of fortitude, the spirit of knowledge, and of godliness.3 And he shall be filled with the spirit of the fear of the Lord. He shall not judge according to the sight of the eyes, nor reprove according to the hearing of the ears.4 But he shall judge the poor with justice, and shall reprove with equity for the meek of the earth: land he shall strike the earth with the rod of his mouth, and with the breath of his lips he shall slay the wicked.5 And justice shall be the girdle of his loins: and faith the girdle of his reins.6 The wolf shall dwell with the lamb: and the leopard shall lie down with the kid: the calf and the lion, and the sheep shall abide together, and a little child shall lead them.7 The calf and the bear shall feed: their young ones shall rest together: and the lion shall eat straw like the ox.8 And the sucking child shall play on the hole of the asp: and the weaned child shall thrust his hand into the den of the basilisk.9 They shall not hurt, nor shall they kill in all my holy mountain, for the earth is filled with the knowledge of the Lord, as the covering waters of the sea.10 In that day the root of Jesse, who standeth for an ensign of the people, him the Gentiles shall beseech, and his sepulchre shall be glorious.

Responsorial Psalm: Psalms 72: 1-2, 7-8, 12-13, 17

R. (7) Justice shall flourish in his time, and fullness of peace for ever.

2 Give to the king thy judgment, O God: and to the king's son thy justice: To judge thy people with justice, and thy poor with judgment.

R. Justice shall flourish in his time, and fullness of peace for ever.

7 In his days shall justice spring up, and abundance of peace, till the moon be taken sway.

8 And he shall rule from sea to sea, and from the river unto the ends of the earth.

R. Justice shall flourish in his time, and fullness of peace for ever.

12 For he shall deliver the poor from the mighty: and the needy that had no helper.

13 He shall spare the poor and needy: and he shall save the souls of the poor.

R. Justice shall flourish in his time, and fullness of peace for ever.

17 Let his name be blessed for evermore: his name continueth before the sun. And in him shall all the tribes of the earth be blessed: all nations shall magnify him.

R. Justice shall flourish in his time, and fullness of peace for ever.

Alleluia

R. Alleluia, alleluia.

Behold, our Lord shall come with power; he will enlighten the eyes of his servants.

R. Alleluia, alleluia.

Gospel: Luke 10: 21-24

21 In that same hour, he rejoiced in the Holy Ghost, and said: I confess to thee, O Father, Lord of heaven and earth, because thou hast hidden these things from the wise and prudent, and hast revealed them to little ones. Yea, Father, for so it hath seemed good in thy sight. 22 All things are delivered to me by my Father; and no one knoweth who the Son is, but the Father; and who the Father is, but the Son, and to whom the Son will reveal him. 23 And turning to his disciples, he said: Blessed are the

eyes that see the things which you see.*24* For I say to you, that many prophets and kings have desired to see the things that you see, and have not seen them; and to hear the things that you hear, and have not heard them.

December 4, 2024

Wednesday of the First Week of Advent

First Reading: Isaiah 25: 6-10a

6 And the Lord of hosts shall make unto all people in this mountain, a feast of fat things, a feast of wine, of fat things full of marrow, of wine purified from the lees.*7* And he shall destroy in this mountain the face of the bond with which all people were tied, and the web that he began over all nations.*8* He shall cast death down headlong for ever: and the Lord God shall wipe away tears from every face, and the reproach of his people he shall take away from off the whole earth: for the Lord hath spoken it.*9* And they shall say in that day: Lo, this is our God, we have waited for him, and he will save us: this is the Lord, we have patiently waited for him, we shall rejoice and be joyfull in his salvation.*10a* For the hand of the Lord shall rest in this mountain.

Responsorial Psalm: Psalms 23: 1-3a, 3b-4, 5, 6

R. (6cd) I shall live in the house of the Lord all the days of my life.

1 The Lord ruleth me: and I shall want nothing.

2 He hath set me in a place of pasture. He hath brought me up, on the water of refreshment:

3a He hath converted my soul.

R. I shall live in the house of the Lord all the days of my life.

3b He hath led me on the paths of justice, for his own name's sake.

4 For though I should walk in the midst of the shadow of death, I will fear no evils, for thou art with me. Thy rod and thy staff, they have comforted me.

R. I shall live in the house of the Lord all the days of my life.

5 Thou hast prepared a table before me against them that afflict me. Thou hast anointed my head with oil; and my chalice which inebriateth me, how goodly is it!

R. I shall live in the house of the Lord all the days of my life.

6 And thy mercy will follow me all the days of my life. And that I may dwell in the house of the Lord unto length of days.

R. I shall live in the house of the Lord all the days of my life.

Alleluia

R. Alleluia, alleluia.

Behold, the Lord comes to save his people; blessed are those prepared to meet him.

R. Alleluia, alleluia.

Gospel: Matthew 15: 29-37

29 And when Jesus had passed away from thence, he came nigh the sea of Galilee. And going up into a mountain, he sat there.*30* And there came to him great multitudes, having with them the dumb, the blind, the lame, the maimed, and many others: and they cast them down at his feet, and he healed them:*31* So that the multitudes marvelled seeing the dumb speak, the lame walk, and the blind see: and they glorified the God of Israel.*32* And Jesus called together his disciples, and said: I have compassion on the multitudes, because they continue with me now three days, and have not what to eat, and I will not send them away fasting, lest they faint in the way.*33* And the disciples say unto him: Whence then should we have so many loaves in the desert, as to fill so great a multitude?*34* And Jesus said to them: How many loaves have you? But they said: Seven, and a few little fishes.*35* And he commanded the multitude to sit down upon the ground.*36* And taking the seven loaves and the fishes, and giving thanks, he brake, and gave to his disciples, and the disciples to the people.*37* And they did all eat, and had their fill. And they took up seven baskets full, of what remained of the fragments.

December 5, 2024

Thursday of the First Week of Advent

First Reading: Isaiah 26: 1-6

1 In that day shall this canticle be sung the land of Juda. Sion the city of our strength a saviour, a wall and a bulwark shall be set therein.*2* Open ye the gates, and let the just nation, that keepeth the truth, enter in.*3* The old error is passed away: thou wilt keep peace: peace, because we have hoped in thee.*4* You have hoped in the Lord for evermore, in the Lord God mighty for ever.*5* For he shall bring down them that dwell on high, the high city he shall lay low. He shall bring it down even to the ground, he shall pull it down even to the dust.*6* The foot shall tread it down, the feet of the poor, the steps of the needy.

Responsorial Psalm: Psalms 118: 1 and 8-9, 19-21, 25-27a

R. (26a) Blessed is he who comes in the name of the Lord.

or

R. Alleluia.

1 Give praise to Lord, for he is good: for his mercy endureth for ever.

8 It is good to confide in the Lord, rather than to have confidence in man.

9 It is good to trust in the Lord, rather than to trust in princes.

R. Blessed is he who comes in the name of the Lord.

or

R. Alleluia.

19 Open ye to me the gates of justice: I will go into them, and give praise to the Lord.

20 This is the gate of the Lord, the just shall enter into it.

21 I will give glory to thee because thou hast heard me: and art become my salvation.

R. Blessed is he who comes in the name of the Lord.

or

R. Alleluia.

25 O Lord, save me: O Lord, give good success.

26 Blessed be he that cometh in the name Lord. We have blessed you out of the house of the Lord.

27a The Lord is God, and he hath shone upon us.

R. Blessed is he who comes in the name of the Lord.

or

R. Alleluia.

Alleluia: Isaiah 55: 6

R. Alleluia, alleluia.

6 Seek the LORD while he may be found; call him while he is near.

R. Alleluia, alleluia.

Gospel: Matthew 7: 21, 24-27

21 Not every one that saith to me, Lord, Lord, shall enter into the kingdom of heaven: but he that doth the will of my Father who is in heaven, he shall enter into the kingdom of heaven.24 Every one therefore that heareth these my words, and doth them, shall be likened to a wise man that built his house upon a rock,25 And the rain fell, and the floods came, and the winds blew, and they beat upon that house, and it fell not, for it was founded on a rock.26 And every one that heareth these my words, and doth them not, shall be like a foolish man that built his house upon the sand,27 And the rain fell, and the floods came, and the winds blew, and they beat upon that house, and it fell, and great was the fall thereof.

December 6, 2024

Friday of the First Week of Advent

First Reading: Isaiah 29: 17-24

17 Is it not yet a very little while, and Libanus shall be turned into charmel, and charmel shall be esteemed as a forest?*18* And in that day the deaf shall hear the words of the book, and out of darkness and obscurity the eyes of the blind shall see.*19* And the meek shall increase their joy in the Lord, and the poor men shall rejoice in the Holy One of Israel.*20* For he that did prevail hath failed, the scorner is consumed, and they are all cut off that watched for iniquity:*21* That made men sin by word, and supplanted him that reproved them in the gate, and declined in vain from the just.*22* Therefore thus saith the Lord to the house of Jacob, he that redeemed Abraham: Jacob shall not now be confounded, neither shall his countenance now be ashamed:*23* But when he shall see his children, the work of my hands in the midst of him sanctifying my name, and they shall sanctify the Holy One of Jacob, and shall glorify the God of Israel:*24* And they that erred in spirit, shall know understanding, and they that murmured, shall learn the law.

Responsorial Psalm: Psalms 27: 1, 4, 13-14

R. (1a) The Lord is my light and my salvation.

1 The psalm of David before he was anointed. The Lord is my light and my salvation, whom shall I fear? The Lord is the protector of my life: of whom shall I be afraid?

R. The Lord is my light and my salvation.

4 One thing I have asked of the Lord, this will I seek after; that I may dwell in the house of the Lord all the days of my life. That I may see the delight of the Lord, and may visit his temple.

R. The Lord is my light and my salvation.

13 I believe to see the good things of the Lord in the land of the living.

14 Expect the Lord, do manfully, and let thy heart take courage, and wait thou for the Lord.

R. The Lord is my light and my salvation.

Alleluia

R. Alleluia, alleluia.

Behold, our Lord shall come with power; he will enlighten the eyes of his servants.

R. Alleluia, alleluia.

Gospel: Matthew 9: 27-31

27 And as Jesus passed from thence, there followed him two blind men crying out and saying, Have mercy on us, O Son of David.28 And when he was come to the house, the blind men came to him. And Jesus saith to them, Do you believe, that I can do this unto you? They say to him, Yea, Lord.29 Then he touched their eyes, saying, According to your faith, be it done unto you.30 And their eyes were opened, and Jesus strictly charged them, saying, See that no man know this.31 But they going out, spread his fame abroad in all that country.

December 7, 2024

Memorial of Saint Ambrose, Bishop and Doctor of the Church

First Reading: Isaiah 30: 19-21, 23-26

19 For the people of Sion shall dwell in Jerusalem: weeping thou shalt not weep, he will surely have pity on thee: at the voice of thy cry, as soon as he shall hear, he will answer thee.20 And the Lord will give you spare bread, and short water: and will not cause thy teacher to flee away from thee any more, and thy eyes shall see thy teacher.21 And thy ears shall hear the word of one admonishing thee behind thy

back: This is the way, walk ye in it: and go not aside neither to the right hand, nor to the left.23 And rain shall be given to thy seed, wheresoever thou shalt sow in the land: and the bread of the corn of the land shall be most plentiful, and fat. The lamb in that day shall feed at large in thy possession:24 And thy oxen, and the ass colts that till the ground, shall eat mingled provender as it was winnowed in the floor.25 And there shall be upon every high mountain, and upon every elevated hill rivers of running waters in the day of the slaughter of many, when the tower shall fall.26 And the light of the moon shall be as the light of the sun, and the light of the sun shall be sevenfold, as the light of seven days: in the day when the Lord shall bind up the wound of his people, and shall heal the stroke of their wound.

Responsorial Psalm: Psalms 147: 1-2, 3-4, 5-6

R. (Isaiah 30:18d) Blessed are all who wait for the Lord.

1 Praise ye the Lord, because psalm is good: to our God be joyful and comely praise.

2 The Lord buildeth up Jerusalem: he will gather together the dispersed of Israel.

R. Blessed are all who wait for the Lord.

3 Who healeth the broken of heart, and bindeth up their bruises.

4 Who telleth the number of the stars: and calleth them all by their names.

R. Blessed are all who wait for the Lord.

5 Great is our Lord, and great is his power: and of his wisdom there is no number.

6 The Lord lifteth up the meek, and bringeth the wicked down even to the ground.

R. Blessed are all who wait for the Lord.

Alleluia: Isaiah 33: 22

R. Alleluia, alleluia.

22 The LORD is our Judge, our Lawgiver, our King; he it is who will save us.

R. Alleluia, alleluia.

Gospel: Matthew 9: 35 – 10: 1, 5a, 6-8

35 And Jesus went about all the cities, and towns, teaching in their synagogues, and preaching the gospel of the kingdom, and healing every disease, and every infirmity.36 And seeing the multitudes, he had compassion on them: because they were distressed, and lying like sheep that have no shepherd.37 Then he saith to his disciples, The harvest indeed is great, but the labourers are few.38 Pray ye therefore the Lord of the harvest, that he send forth labourers into his harvest.10:1 And having called his twelve disciples together, he gave them power over unclean spirits, to cast them out, and to heal all manner of diseases, and all manner of infirmities.5a These twelve Jesus sent: commanding them, saying:6 But go ye rather to the lost sheep of the house of Israel.7 And going, preach, saying: The kingdom of heaven is at hand.8 Heal the sick, raise the dead, cleanse the lepers, cast out devils: freely have you received, freely give.

December 8, 2024

Second Sunday of Advent

First Reading: Baruch 5: 1-9

1 Put off, O Jerusalem, the garment of thy mourning, and affliction: and put on the beauty, and honour of that everlasting glory which thou hast from God.2 God will clothe thee with the double garment of justice, and will set a crown on thy head of

everlasting honour.*3* For God will shew his brightness in thee, to every one under heaven.*4* For thy name shall be named to thee by God for ever: the peace of justice, and honour of piety.*5* Arise, O Jerusalem, and stand on high: and look about towards the east, and behold thy children gathered together from the rising to the setting sun, by the word of the Holy One rejoicing in the remembrance of God.*6* For they went out from thee on foot, led by the enemies: but the Lord will bring them to thee exalted with honour as children of the kingdom.*7* For God hath appointed to bring down every high mountain, and the everlasting rocks, and to fill up the valleys to make them even with the ground: that Israel may walk diligently to the honour of God.*8* Moreover the woods, and every sweet-smelling tree have overshadowed Israel by the commandment of God.*9* For God will bring Israel with joy in the light of his majesty, with mercy, and justice, that cometh from him.

Responsorial Psalm: Psalms 126: 1-2, 2-3, 4-5, 6

R. (3) The Lord has done great things for us; we are filled with joy.

1 When the lord brought back the captivity of Sion, we became like men comforted.

2ab Then was our mouth filled with gladness; and our tongue with joy.

R. The Lord has done great things for us; we are filled with joy.

2cd Then shall they say among the Gentiles: The Lord hath done great things for them.

3 The Lord hath done great things for us: we are become joyful.

R. The Lord has done great things for us; we are filled with joy.

4 Turn again our captivity, O Lord, as a stream in the south.

5 They that sow in tears shall reap in joy.

R. The Lord has done great things for us; we are filled with joy.

6 Going they went and wept, casting their seeds. But coming they shall come with joyfulness, carrying their sheaves.

R. The Lord has done great things for us; we are filled with joy.

Second Reading: Philippians 1: 4-6, 8-11

4 Always in all my prayers making supplication for you all, with joy;*5* For your communication in the gospel of Christ from the first day until now.*6* Being confident of this very thing, that he, who hath begun a good work in you, will perfect it unto the day of Christ Jesus.*8* For God is my witness, how I long after you all in the bowels of Jesus Christ.*9* And this I pray, that your charity may more and more abound in knowledge, and in all understanding:*10* That you may approve the better things, that you may be sincere and without offence unto the day of Christ,*11* Filled with the fruit of justice, through Jesus Christ, unto the glory and praise of God.

Alleluia: Luke 3: 4, 6

R. Alleluia, alleluia.

4, 6 Prepare the way of the Lord, make straight his paths: all flesh shall see the salvation of God.

R. Alleluia, alleluia.

Gospel: Luke 3: 1-6

1 Now in the fifteenth year of the reign of Tiberius Caesar, Pontius Pilate being governor of Judea, and Herod being tetrarch of Galilee, and Philip his brother tetrarch of Iturea, and the country of Trachonitis, and Lysanias tetrarch of Abilina;2 Under the high priests Annas and Caiphas; the word of the Lord was made unto John, the son of Zachary, in the desert.3 And he came into all the country about the Jordan, preaching the baptism of penance for the remission of sins;4 As it was written in the book of the sayings of Isaias the prophet: A voice of one crying in the wilderness: Prepare ye the way of the Lord, make straight his paths.5 Every valley shall be filled; and every mountain and hill shall be brought low; and the crooked shall be made straight; and the rough ways plain;6 And all flesh shall see the salvation of God.

December 9, 2024

Solemnity of the Immaculate Conception of the Blessed Virgin Mary

First Reading: Genesis 3: 9-15, 20

9 And the Lord God called Adam, and said to him: Where art thou?10 And he said: I heard thy voice in paradise; and I was afraid, because I was naked, and I hid myself.11 And he said to him: And who hath told thee that thou wast naked, but that thou hast eaten of the tree whereof I commanded thee that thou shouldst not eat?12 And Adam said: The woman, whom thou gavest me to be my companion, gave me of the tree, and I did eat.13 And the Lord God said to the woman: Why hast thou done this? And she answered: The serpent deceived me, and I did eat.14 And the Lord God said to the serpent: Because thou hast done this thing, thou art cursed among all cattle, and beasts of the earth: upon thy breast shalt thou go, and earth shalt thou eat all the days of thy life.15 I will put enmities between thee and the woman, and thy seed and her seed: she shall crush thy head, and thou shalt lie in wait for her heel.20 And Adam called the name of his wife Eve: because she was the mother of all the living.

Responsorial Psalm: Psalms 98: 1, 2-3ab, 3cd-4

R. (1) Sing to the Lord a new song, for he has done marvelous deeds.

1 Sing ye to the Lord anew canticle: because he hath done wonderful things. His right hand hath wrought for him salvation, and his arm is holy.

R. Sing to the Lord a new song, for he has done marvelous deeds.

2 The Lord hath made known his salvation: he hath revealed his justice in the sight of the Gentiles.

3ab He hath remembered his mercy his truth toward the house of Israel.

R. Sing to the Lord a new song, for he has done marvelous deeds.

3cd All the ends of the earth have seen the salvation of our God.

4 Sing joyfully to God, all the earth; make melody, rejoice and sing.

R. Sing to the Lord a new song, for he has done marvelous deeds.

Second Reading: Ephesians 1: 3-6, 11-12

3 Blessed be the God and Father of our Lord Jesus Christ, who hath blessed us with spiritual blessings in heavenly places, in Christ:*4* As he chose us in him before the foundation of the world, that we should be holy and unspotted in his sight in charity.*5* Who hath predestinated us unto the adoption of children through Jesus Christ unto himself: according to the purpose of his will:*6* Unto the praise of the glory of his grace, in which he hath graced us in his beloved son.*11* In whom we also are called by lot, being predestinated according to the purpose of him who worketh all things according to the counsel of his will.*12* That we may be unto the praise of his glory, we who before hoped Christ:

Alleluia: Luke 1: 28

R. Alleluia, alleluia.

28 Hail, Mary, full of grace, the Lord is with you; blessed are you among women.

R. Alleluia, alleluia.

Gospel: Luke 1: 26-38

26 And in the sixth month, the angel Gabriel was sent from God into a city of Galilee, called Nazareth,*27* To a virgin espoused to a man whose name was Joseph, of the house of David; and the virgin's name was Mary.*28* And the angel being come in, said unto her: Hail, full of grace, the Lord is with thee: blessed art thou among women.*29* Who having heard, was troubled at his saying, and thought with herself what manner of salutation this should be.*30* And the angel said to her: Fear not, Mary, for thou hast found grace with God.*31* Behold thou shalt conceive in thy womb, and shalt bring forth a son; and thou shalt call his name Jesus.*32* He shall be great, and shall be called the Son of the most High; and the Lord God shall give unto him the throne of David his father; and he shall reign in the house of Jacob for ever.*33* And of his kingdom there shall be no end.*34* And Mary said to the angel: How shall this be done, because I know not man?*35* And the angel answering, said to her: The Holy Ghost shall come upon thee, and the power of the most High shall overshadow thee. And therefore also the Holy which shall be born of thee shall be called the Son of God.*36* And behold thy cousin Elizabeth, she also hath conceived a son in her old age; and this is the sixth month with her that is called barren:*37* Because no word shall be impossible with God.*38* And Mary said: Behold the handmaid of the Lord; be it done to me according to thy word. And the angel departed from her.

December 10, 2024

Tuesday of the Second Week of Advent

First Reading: Isaiah 40: 1-11

1 Be comforted, be comforted, my people, saith your God.*2* Speak ye to the heart of Jerusalem, and call to her: for her evil is come to an end, her iniquity is forgiven: she hath received of the hand of the Lord double for all her sins.*3* The voice of one crying in the desert: Prepare ye the way of the Lord, make straight in the wilderness the paths of our God.*4* Every valley shall be exalted, and every mountain and hill shall be made low, and the crooked shall become straight, and the rough ways plain.*5* And the glory of the Lord shall be revealed, and all flesh together shall see, that the mouth of the Lord hath spoken.*6* The voice of one, saying: Cry. And I said: What shall I cry? All flesh is grass, and all the glory thereof as the flower of the held.*7* The grass is withered, and the dower is fallen, because the spirit of the Lord hath blown upon it. Indeed the people is grass:*8* The grass is withered, and the flower is fallen: but the word of our Lord endureth for ever.*9* Get thee up upon a high mountain, thou that bringest good tidings to Sion: lift up thy voice with strength, thou that bringest good tidings to Jerusalem: lift it up, fear not. Say to the cities of Juda: Behold your God:*10* Behold the Lord God shall come with strength, and his arm shall rule: Behold his reward is with him and his work is before him.*11* He shall feed his flock like a shepherd: he shall gather together the lambs with his arm, and shall take them up in his bosom, and he himself shall carry them that are with young.

Responsorial Psalm: Psalms 96: 1-2, 3 and 10ac, 11-12, 13

R. (Isaiah 40:10ab) The Lord our God comes with power.

1 Sing ye to the Lord a new canticle: sing to the Lord, all the earth.

2 Sing ye to the Lord and bless his name: shew forth his salvation from day to day.

R. The Lord our God comes with power.

3 Declare his glory among the Gentiles: his wonders among all people.

10 Say ye among the Gentiles, the Lord hath reigned. he will judge the people with justice.

R. The Lord our God comes with power.

11 Let the heavens rejoice, and let the earth be glad, let the sea be moved, and the fulness thereof:

12 The fields and all things that are in them shall be joyful. Then shall all the trees of the woods rejoice

R. The Lord our God comes with power.

13 Before the face of the Lord, because he cometh: because he cometh to judge the earth. He shall judge the world with justice, and the people with his truth.

R. The Lord our God comes with power.

Alleluia

R. Alleluia, alleluia.

The day of the Lord is near; Behold, he comes to save us.

R. Alleluia, alleluia.

Gospel: Matthew 18: 12-14

12 What think you? If a man have an hundred sheep, and one of them should go astray: doth he not leave the ninety-nine in the mountains, and go to seek that which is gone astray?*13* And if it so be that he find it: Amen I say to you, he rejoiceth more for that, than for the ninety-nine that went not astray.*14* Even so it is not the will of your Father, who is in heaven, that one of these little ones should perish.

December 11, 2024

Wednesday of the Second Week of Advent

First Reading: Isaiah 40: 25-31

25 And to whom have ye likened me, or made me equal, saith the Holy One?*26* Lift up your eyes on high, and see who hath created these things: who bringeth out their host by number, and calleth them all by their names: by the greatness of his might, and strength, and power, not one of them was missing.*27* Why sayest thou, O Jacob, and speakest, O Israel: My way is hid from the Lord, and my judgment is passed over from my God?*28* Knowest thou not, or hast thou not heard? the Lord is the everlasting God, who hath created the ends of the earth: he shall not faint, nor labour, neither is there any searching out of his wisdom.*29* It is he that giveth strength to the weary, and increaseth force and might to them that are not.*30* Youths shall faint, and labour, and young men shall fall by infirmity.*31* But they that hope in the Lord shall renew their strength, they shall take wings as eagles, they shall run and not be weary, they shall walk and not faint.

Responsorial Psalm: Psalms 103: 1-2, 3-4, 8 and 10

R. (1) O bless the Lord, my soul!

1 Bless the Lord, O my soul: and let all that is within me bless his holy name.

2 Bless the Lord, O my soul, and never forget all he hath done for thee.

R. O bless the Lord, my soul!

3 Who forgiveth all thy iniquities: who healeth all thy diseases.

4 Who redeemeth thy life from destruction: who crowneth thee with mercy and compassion.

R. O bless the Lord, my soul!

8 The Lord is compassionate and merciful: longsuffering and plenteous in mercy.

10 He hath not dealt with us according to our sins: nor rewarded us according to our iniquities.

R. O bless the Lord, my soul!

Alleluia

R. Alleluia, alleluia.

Behold, the Lord comes to save his people; blessed are those prepared to meet him.

R. Alleluia, alleluia.

Gospel: Matthew 11: 28-30

28 Come to me, all you that labour, and are burdened, and I will refresh you.*29* Take up my yoke upon you, and learn of me, because I am meek, and humble of heart: and you shall find rest to your souls.*30* For my yoke is sweet and my burden light.

December 12, 2024

Feast of Our Lady of Guadalupe

First Reading: Zechariah 2: 14-17 or Revelation 11: 19a; 12: 1-6a, 10ab

14 Sing praise, and rejoice, O daughter of Sion: for behold I come, and I will dwell in the midst of thee: saith the Lord.15 And many nations shall be joined to the Lord in that day, and they shall be my people, and I will dwell in the midst of thee: and thou shalt know that the Lord of hosts hath sent me to thee.16 And the Lord shall possess Juda his portion in the sanctified land: and he shall yet choose Jerusalem.17 Let all flesh be silent at the presence of the Lord: for he is risen up out of his. holy habitation.

Or

19a And the temple of God was opened in heaven: and the ark of his testament was seen in his temple1 And a great sign appeared in heaven: A woman clothed with the sun, and the moon under her feet, and on her head a crown of twelve stars:2 And being with child, she cried travailing in birth, and was in pain to be delivered.3 And there was seen another sign in heaven: and behold a great red dragon, having seven heads, and ten horns: and on his head seven diadems:4 And his tail drew the third part of the stars of heaven, and cast them to the earth: and the dragon stood before the woman who was ready to be delivered; that, when she should be delivered, he might devour her son.5 And she brought forth a man child, who was to rule all nations with an iron rod: and her son was taken up to God, and to his throne.6a And the woman fled into the wilderness, where she had a place prepared by God.10ab And I heard a loud voice in heaven, saying: Now is come salvation, and strength, and the kingdom of our God, and the power of his Christ.

Responsorial Psalm: Judith 13: 18bcde, 19

R. (15:9d) You are the highest honor of our race.

18bcde Blessed art thou, O daughter, by the Lord the most high God, above all women upon the earth. Blessed be the Lord who made heaven and earth.

R. You are the highest honor of our race.

19 And all the people said: So be it, so be it. And Achior being called for came, and Judith said to him: The God of Israel, to whom thou gavest testimony, that he revengeth himself of his enemies, he hath cut off the head of all the unbelievers this night by my hand.

R. You are the highest honor of our race.

Alleluia

R. Alleluia, alleluia.

Blessed are you, holy Virgin Mary, deserving of all praise; from you rose the sun of justice, Christ our God.

R. Alleluia, alleluia.

Gospel: Luke 1: 26-38 or Luke 1: 39-47

26 And in the sixth month, the angel Gabriel was sent from God into a city of Galilee, called Nazareth,*27* To a virgin espoused to a man whose name was Joseph, of the house of David; and the virgin's name was Mary.*28* And the angel being come in, said unto her: Hail, full of grace, the Lord is with thee: blessed art thou among women.*29* Who having heard, was troubled at his saying, and thought with herself what manner of salutation this should be.*30* And the angel said to her: Fear not, Mary, for thou hast found grace with God.*31* Behold thou shalt conceive in thy womb, and shalt bring forth a son; and thou shalt call his name Jesus.*32* He shall be great, and shall be called the Son of the most High; and the Lord God shall give unto him the throne of

David his father; and he shall reign in the house of Jacob for ever.*33* And of his kingdom there shall be no end.*34* And Mary said to the angel: How shall this be done, because I know not man?*35* And the angel answering, said to her: The Holy Ghost shall come upon thee, and the power of the most High shall overshadow thee. And therefore also the Holy which shall be born of thee shall be called the Son of God.*36* And behold thy cousin Elizabeth, she also hath conceived a son in her old age; and this is the sixth month with her that is called barren:*37* Because no word shall be impossible with God.*38* And Mary said: Behold the handmaid of the Lord; be it done to me according to thy word. And the angel departed from her.

Or

39 And Mary rising up in those days, went into the hill country with haste into a city of Juda.*40* And she entered into the house of Zachary, and saluted Elizabeth.*41* And it came to pass, that when Elizabeth heard the salutation of Mary, the infant leaped in her womb. And Elizabeth was filled with the Holy Ghost:*42* And she cried out with a loud voice, and said: Blessed art thou among women, and blessed is the fruit of thy womb.*43* And whence is this to me, that the mother of my Lord should come to me?*44* For behold as soon as the voice of thy salutation sounded in my ears, the infant in my womb leaped for joy.*45* And blessed art thou that hast believed, because those things shall be accomplished that were spoken to thee by the Lord.*46* And Mary said: My soul doth magnify the Lord.*47* And my spirit hath rejoiced in God my Saviour.

December 13, 2024

Memorial of Saint Lucy, Virgin and Martyr

First Reading: Isaiah 48: 17-19

17 Thus saith the Lord thy redeemer, the Holy One of Israel: I am the Lord thy God that teach thee profitable things, that govern thee in the way that thou walkest.*18* O that thou hadst hearkened to my commandments: thy peace had been as a river, and thy justice as the waves of the sea,*19* And thy seed had been as the sand, and the offspring of thy bowels like the gravel thereof: his name should not have perished, nor have been destroyed from before my face.

Responsorial Psalm: Psalms 1: 1-2, 3, 4 and 6

R. (John 8:12) Those who follow you, Lord, will have the light of life.

1 Blessed is the man who hath not walked in the counsel of the ungodly, nor stood in the way of sinners, nor sat in the chair of pestilence.

2 But his will is in the law of the Lord, and on his law he shall meditate day and night.

R. Those who follow you, Lord, will have the light of life.

3 And he shall be like a tree which is planted near the running waters, which shall bring forth its fruit, in due season. And his leaf shall not fall off: and all whatsoever he shall do shall prosper.

R. Those who follow you, Lord, will have the light of life.

4 Not so the wicked, not so: but like the dust, which the wind driveth from the face of the earth.

6 For the Lord knoweth the way of the just: and the way of the wicked shall perish.

R. Those who follow you, Lord, will have the light of life.

Alleluia

R. Alleluia, alleluia.

The Lord will come; go out to meet him! He is the prince of peace.

R. Alleluia, alleluia.

Gospel: Matthew 11: 16-19

16 But whereunto shall I esteem this generation to be like? It is like to children sitting in the market place.*17* Who crying to their companions say: We have piped to you, and you have not danced: we have lamented, and you have not mourned.*18* For John came neither eating nor drinking; and they say: He hath a devil.*19* The Son of man came eating and drinking, and they say: Behold a man that is a glutton and a wine drinker, a friend of publicans and sinners. And wisdom is justified by her children.

December 14, 2024

Memorial of Saint John of the Cross, Priest and Doctor of the Church

First Reading: Sirach 48: 1-4, 9-11

1 And Elias the prophet stood up, as a fire, and his word burnt like a torch.*2* He brought a famine upon them, and they that provoked him in their envy, were reduced to a small number, for they could not endure the commandments of the Lord.*3* By the word of the Lord he shut up the heaven, and he brought down fire from heaven thrice.*4* Thus was Elias magnified in his wondrous works. And who can glory like to thee?*9* Who wast taken up in a whirlwind of fire, in a chariot of fiery horses.*10* Who art registered in the judgments of times to appease the wrath of the Lord, to reconcile the heart of the father to the son, and to restore the tribes of Jacob.*11* Blessed are they that saw thee, and were honoured with thy friendship.

Responsorial Psalm: Psalms 80: 2ac and 3b, 15-16, 18-19

R. (4) Lord, make us turn to you; let us see your face and we shall be saved.

2ac Give ear, O thou that rulest Israel: Thou that sittest upon the cherubims, shine forth

3b Stir up thy might.

R. Lord, make us turn to you; let us see your face and we shall be saved.

15 Turn again, O God of hosts, look down from heaven, and see, and visit this vineyard:

16 And perfect the same which thy right hand hath planted: and upon the son of man whom thou hast confirmed for thyself.

R. Lord, make us turn to you; let us see your face and we shall be saved.

18 Let thy hand be upon the man of thy right hand: and upon the son of man whom thou hast confirmed for thyself.

19 And we depart not from thee, thou shalt quicken us: and we will call upon thy name.

R. Lord, make us turn to you; let us see your face and we shall be saved.

Alleluia: Luke 3: 4, 6

R. Alleluia, alleluia.

4, 6 Prepare the way of the Lord, make straight his paths: All flesh shall see the salvation of God.

R. Alleluia, alleluia.

Gospel: Matthew 17: 9a, 10-13

9 And as they came down from the mountain, Jesus charged them, saying: Tell the vision to no man, till the Son of man be risen from the dead.*10* And his disciples asked him, saying: Why then do the scribes say that Elias must come first?*11* But he answering, said to them: Elias indeed shall come, and restore all things.*12* But I say to you, that Elias is already come, and they knew him not, but have done unto him whatsoever they had a mind. So also the Son of man shall suffer from them.*13* Then the disciples understood, that he had spoken to them of John the Baptist.

December 15, 2024

Third Sunday of Advent

First Reading: Zephaniah 3: 14-18a

14 Give praise, O daughter of Sion: shout, O Israel: be glad, and rejoice with all thy heart, O daughter of Jerusalem.*15* The Lord hath taken away thy judgment, he hath turned away thy enemies: the king of Israel the Lord is in the midst of thee, thou shalt fear evil no more.*16* In that day it shall be said to Jerusalem: Fear not: to Sion: Let not thy hands be weakened.*17* The Lord thy God in the midst of thee is mighty, he will save: he will rejoice over thee with gladness, he will be silent in his love, he will be joyful over thee in praise.*18a* The triflers that were departed from the law, I will gather together.

Responsorial Psalm: Isaiah 12: 2-3, 4, 5-6

R. (6) Cry out with joy and gladness: for among you is the great and Holy One of Israel.

2 Behold, God is my saviour, I will deal confidently, and will not fear: O because the Lord is my strength, and my praise, and he is become my salvation.

3 You shall draw waters with joy out of the saviour's fountains:

R. Cry out with joy and gladness: for among you is the great and Holy One of Israel.

4 And you shall say in that day: Praise ye the Lord, and call upon his name: make his works known among the people: remember that his name is high.

R. Cry out with joy and gladness: for among you is the great and Holy One of Israel.

5 Sing ye to the Lord, for he hath done great things: shew this forth in all the earth.

6 Rejoice, and praise, O thou habitation of Sion: for great is he that is in the midst of thee, the Holy One of Israel.

R. Cry out with joy and gladness: for among you is the great and Holy One of Israel.

Second Reading: Philippians 4: 4-7

4 Rejoice in the Lord always; again, I say, rejoice.*5* Let your modesty be known to all men. The Lord is nigh.*6* Be nothing solicitous; but in every thing, by prayer and supplication, with thanksgiving, let your petitions be made known to God.*7* And the peace of God, which surpasseth all understanding, keep your hearts and minds in Christ Jesus.

Alleluia: Isaiah 61: 1

R. Alleluia, alleluia.

1 The Spirit of the Lord is upon me, because he has anointed me to bring glad tidings to the poor.

R. Alleluia, alleluia.

Gospel: Luke 3: 10-18

10 And the people asked him, saying: What then shall we do?*11* And he answering, said to them: He that hath two coats, let him give to him that hath none; and he that hath meat, let him do in like manner.*12* And the publicans also came to be baptized, and said to him: Master, what shall we do?*13* But he said to them: Do nothing more than that which is appointed you.*14* And the soldiers also asked him, saying: And what shall we do? And he said to them: Do violence to no man; neither calumniate any man; and be content with your pay.*15* And as the people were of opinion, and all were thinking in their hearts of John, that perhaps he might be the Christ;*16* John answered, saying unto all: I indeed baptize you with water; but there shall come one mightier than I, the latchet of whose shoes I am not worthy to loose: he shall baptize you with the Holy Ghost, and with fire:*17* Whose fan is in his hand, and he will purge his floor, and will gather the wheat into his barn; but the chaff he will burn with unquenchable fire.*18* And many other things exhorting, did he preach to the people.

December 16, 2024

Monday of the Third Week of Advent

First Reading: Numbers 24: 2-7, 15-17

2 And lifting up his eyes, he saw Israel abiding in their tents by their tribes: and the spirit of God rushing upon him,*3* He took up his parable and said: Balaam the son of Beor hath said: The man hath said, whose eye ire stopped up:*4* The hearer of the words of God hath said, he that hath beheld the vision of the Almighty, he that falleth, and so his eyes are opened:*5* How beautiful are thy tabernacles, O Jacob, and thy tents, O Israel!*6* As woody valleys, as watered gardens near the rivers, as tabernacles which the Lord hath pitched, as cedars by the waterside.*7* Water shall flow out of his bucket, and his seed shall be in many waters. For Agag his king shall be removed, and his kingdom shall be taken awry.*15* Therefore taking up his parable, again he said: Balaam the son of Beor hath said: The man whose eye is stopped up, hath said:*16* The hearer of the words of God hath said, who knoweth the doctrine of the Highest, and seeth the visions of the Almighty, who falling hath his eyes opened:*17* I shall see him, but not now: I shall behold him, but not near. A STAR SHALL RISE out of Jacob and a sceptre shall spring up from Israel.

Responsorial Psalm: Psalms 25: 4-5ab, 6 and 7bc, 8-9

R. (4) Teach me your ways, O Lord.

4 Let all them be confounded that act unjust things without cause. shew, O Lord, thy ways to me, and teach me thy paths.

5ab Direct me in thy truth, and teach me; for thou art God my Saviour.

R. Teach me your ways, O Lord.

6 Remember, O Lord, thy bowels of compassion; and thy mercies that are from the beginning of the world.

7bc According to thy mercy remember thou me: for thy goodness' sake, O Lord.

R. Teach me your ways, O Lord.

8 The Lord is sweet and righteous: therefore he will give a law to sinners in the way.

9 He will guide the mild in judgment: he will teach the meek his ways.

R. Teach me your ways, O Lord.

Alleluia: Psalms 85: 8

R. Alleluia, alleluia.

8 Show us, LORD, your love, and grant us your salvation.

R. Alleluia, alleluia.

Gospel: Matthew 21: 23-27

23 And when he was come into the temple, there came to him, as he was teaching, the chief priests and ancients of the people, saying: By what authority dost thou these things? and who hath given thee this authority?24 Jesus answering, said to them: I also will ask you one word, which if you shall tell me, I will also tell you by what authority I do these things.25 The baptism of John, whence was it? from heaven or from men? But they thought within themselves, saying:26 If we shall say, from heaven, he will say to us: Why then did you not believe him? But if we shall say, from men, we are afraid of the multitude: for all held John as a prophet.27 And answering Jesus, they said: We know not. He also said to them: Neither do I tell you by what authority I do these things.

December 17, 2024

Tuesday of the Third Week of Advent

First Reading: Genesis 49: 2, 8-10

2 Gather yourselves together, and hear, O ye sons of Jacob, hearken to Israel your father:8 Juda, thee shall thy brethren praise: thy hands shall be on the necks of thy enemies: the sons of thy father shall bow down to thee.9 Juda is a lion's whelp: to the prey, my son, thou art gone up: resting thou hast couched as a lion, and as a lioness, who shall rouse him?10 The sceptre shall not be taken away from Juda, nor a ruler from his thigh, till he come that is to be sent, and he shall be the expectation of nations.

Responsorial Psalm: Psalms 72: 1-2, 3-4ab, 7-8, 17

R. (7) Justice shall flourish in his time, and fullness of peace for ever.

1, 2 Give to the king thy judgment, O God: and to the king's son thy justice: To judge thy people with justice, and thy poor with judgment.

R. Justice shall flourish in his time, and fullness of peace for ever.

3 Let the mountains receive peace for the people: and the hills justice.

4ab He shall judge the poor of the people, and he shall save the children of the poor.

R. Justice shall flourish in his time, and fullness of peace for ever.

7 In his days shall justice spring up, and abundance of peace, till the moon be taken sway.

8 And he shall rule from sea to sea, and from the river unto the ends of the earth.

R. Justice shall flourish in his time, and fullness of peace for ever.

17 Let his name be blessed for evermore: his name continueth before the sun. And in him shall all the tribes of the earth be blessed: all nations shall magnify him.

R. Justice shall flourish in his time, and fullness of peace for ever.

Alleluia

R. Alleluia, alleluia.

O Wisdom of our God Most High, guiding creation with power and love: come to teach us the path of knowledge!

R. Alleluia, alleluia.

Gospel: Matthew 1: 1-17

1 The book of the generation of Jesus Christ, the son of David, the son of Abraham:*2* Abraham begot Isaac. And Isaac begot Jacob. And Jacob begot Judas and his brethren.*3* And Judas begot Phares and Zara of Thamar. And Phares begot Esron. And Esron begot Aram.*4* And Aram begot Aminadab. And Aminadab begot Naasson. And Naasson begot Salmon.*5* And Salmon begot Booz of Rahab. And Booz begot Obed of Ruth. And Obed begot Jesse.*6* And Jesse begot David the king. And David the king begot Solomon, of her that had been the wife of Urias.*7* And Solomon begot Roboam. And Roboam begot Abia. And Abia begot Asa.*8* And Asa begot Josaphat. And Josaphat begot Joram. And Joram begot Ozias.*9* And Ozias begot Joatham. And Joatham begot Achaz. And Achaz begot Ezechias.*10* And Ezechias begot Manasses. And Manasses begot Amon. And Amon begot Josias.*11* And Josias begot Jechonias and his brethren in the transmigration of Babylon.*12* And after the transmigration of Babylon, Jechonias begot Salathiel. And Salathiel begot Zorobabel.*13* And Zorobabel begot Abiud. And Abiud begot Eliacim. And Eliacim begot Azor.*14* And Azor begot Sadoc. And Sadoc begot Achim. And Achim begot Eliud.*15* And Eliud begot Eleazar. And Eleazar begot Mathan. And Mathan begot Jacob.*16* And Jacob begot Joseph the husband of Mary, of whom was born Jesus, who is called Christ.*17* So all the generations, from Abraham to David, are fourteen generations. And from David to the transmigration of Babylon, are fourteen generations: and from the transmigration of Babylon to Christ are fourteen generations.

December 18, 2024

Wednesday of the Third Week of Advent

First Reading: Jeremiah 23: 5-8

5 Behold the days come, saith the Lord, and I will raise up to David a just branch: and a king shall reign, and shall be wise, and shall execute judgement and justice in the earth.6 In those days shall Juda be saved, and Israel shall dwell confidently: and this is the name that they shall call him: the Lord our just one.7 Therefore behold the days to come, saith the Lord, and they shall say no more: The Lord liveth, who brought up the children of Israel out of the land of Egypt:8 But the Lord liveth, who hath brought out, and brought hither the seed of the house of Israel from the land of the north, and out of all the lands, to which I had cast them forth: and they shall dwell in their own land.

Responsorial Psalm: Psalms 72: 1-2, 12-13, 18-19

R. (7) Justice shall flourish in his time, and fullness of peace for ever.

1, 2 Give to the king thy judgment, O God: and to the king's son thy justice: To judge thy people with justice, and thy poor with judgment.

R. Justice shall flourish in his time, and fullness of peace for ever.

12 For he shall deliver the poor from the mighty: and the needy that had no helper.

13 He shall spare the poor and needy: and he shall save the souls of the poor.

R. Justice shall flourish in his time, and fullness of peace for ever.

18 Blessed be the Lord, the God of Israel, who alone doth wonderful things.

19 And blessed be the name of his majesty for ever: and the whole earth shall be filled with his majesty. So be it. So be it.

R. Justice shall flourish in his time, and fullness of peace for ever.

Alleluia

R. Alleluia, alleluia.

O Leader of the House of Israel, giver of the Law to Moses on Sinai: come to rescue us with your mighty power!

R. Alleluia, alleluia.

Gospel: Matthew 1: 18-25

18 Now the generation of Christ was in this wise. When as his mother Mary was espoused to Joseph, before they came together, she was found with child, of the Holy Ghost. 19 Whereupon Joseph her husband, being a just man, and not willing publicly to expose her, was minded to put her away privately. 20 But while he thought on these things, behold the angel of the Lord appeared to him in his sleep, saying: Joseph, son of David, fear not to take unto thee Mary thy wife, for that which is conceived in her, is of the Holy Ghost. 21 And she shall bring forth a son: and thou shalt call his name JESUS. For he shall save his people from their sins. 22 Now all this was done that it might be fulfilled which the Lord spoke by the prophet, saying: 23 Behold a virgin shall be with child, and bring forth a son, and they shall call his name Emmanuel, which being interpreted is, God with us. 24 And Joseph rising up from sleep, did as the angel of the Lord had commanded him, and took unto him his wife. 25 And he knew her not till she brought forth her firstborn son: and he called his name JESUS.

December 19, 2024

Thursday of the Third Week of Advent

First Reading: Judges 13: 2-7, 24-25a

2 Now there was a certain man of Saraa, and of the race of Dan, whose name was Manue, and his wife was barren.*3* And an angel of the Lord appeared to her, and said: Thou art barren and without children: but thou shalt conceive and bear a son.*4* Now therefore beware and drink no wine nor strong drink, and eat not any unclean thing.*5* Because thou shalt conceive and bear a son, and no razor shall touch his head: for he shall be a Nazarite of God, from his infancy, and from his mother's womb, and he shall begin to deliver Israel from the hands of the Philistines.*6* And when she was come to her husband she said to him: A man of God came to me, having the countenance of an angel, very awful. And when I asked him who he was, and whence he came, and by what name he was called, he would not tell me.*7* But he answered thus: Behold thou shalt conceive and bear a son: beware thou drink no wine, nor strong drink, nor eat any unclean thing: for the child shall be a Nazarite of God from his infancy, from his mother's womb until the day of his death.*24* And she bore a son, and called his name Samson. And the child grew, and the Lord blessed him.*25a* And the spirit of the Lord began to be with him.

Responsorial Psalm: Psalms 71: 3-4a, 5-6ab, 16-17

R. (8) My mouth shall be filled with your praise, and I will sing your glory!

3 Be thou unto me a God, a protector, and a place of strength: that thou mayst make me safe. For thou art my firmament and my refuge.

4a Deliver me, O my God, out of the hand of the sinner.

R. My mouth shall be filled with your praise, and I will sing your glory!

5 For thou art my patience, O Lord: my hope, O Lord, from my youth;

6ab By thee have I been confirmed from the womb: from my mother's womb thou art my protector.

R. My mouth shall be filled with your praise, and I will sing your glory!

16 I will enter into the powers of the Lord: O Lord, I will be mindful of thy justice alone.

17 Thou hast taught me, O God, from my youth: and till now I will declare thy wonderful works.

R. My mouth shall be filled with your praise, and I will sing your glory!

Alleluia

R. Alleluia, alleluia.

O Root of Jesse's stem, sign of God's love for all his people: come to save us without delay!

R. Alleluia, alleluia.

Gospel: Luke 1: 5-25

5 There was in the days of Herod, the king of Judea, a certain priest named Zachary, of the course of Abia; and his wife was of the daughters of Aaron, and her name Elizabeth.*6* And they were both just before God, walking in all the commandments and justifications of the Lord without blame.*7* And they had no son, for that Elizabeth was barren, and they both were well advanced in years.*8* And it came to pass, when he executed the priestly function in the order of his course before God,*9* According to the custom of the priestly office, it was his lot to offer incense, going into the temple of the Lord.*10* And all the multitude of the people was praying without, at the hour of incense.*11* And there appeared to him an angel of the Lord, standing on the right side of the alter of incense.*12* And Zachary seeing him, was troubled, and fear fell upon him.*13* But the angel said to him: Fear not, Zachary, for thy prayer is heard; and thy wife Elizabeth shall bear thee a son, and thou shalt call his name John:*14* And thou shalt have joy and gladness, and many shall rejoice in his nativity.*15* For he shall be great before the Lord; and shall drink no wine nor strong drink: and he shall be filled with the Holy Ghost, even from his mother's womb.*16* And he shall convert many of the children of Israel to the Lord their God.*17* And he shall go before him in the spirit and power of Elias; that he may turn the hearts of the fathers unto the children, and the incredulous to the wisdom of the just, to prepare unto the Lord a perfect people.*18* And Zachary said to the angel: Whereby shall I know this? for I am an old man, and my wife is advanced in years.*19* And the angel answering, said to him: I am Gabriel, who stand before God: and am sent to speak to thee, and to bring thee these good tidings.*20* And behold, thou shalt be dumb, and shalt not be able to speak until the day wherein these things shall come to pass, because thou hast not believed my words, which shall be fulfilled in their time.*21* And the people were waiting for Zachary; and they wondered that he tarried so long in the temple.*22* And when he came out, he could not speak to them: and they understood that he had seen a vision in the temple. And he made signs to them, and remained dumb.*23* And it came to pass, after the days of his office were accomplished, he departed to his own house.*24* And after those days, Elizabeth his wife conceived, and hid herself five months, saying:*25* Thus hath the Lord dealt with me in the days wherein he hath had regard to take away my reproach among men.

December 20, 2024

Friday of the Third Week of Advent

First Reading: Isaiah 7: 10-14

10 And the Lord spoke again to Achaz, saying:*11* Ask thee a sign of the Lord thy God either unto the depth of hell, or unto the height above.*12* And Achaz said: I will not ask, and I will not tempt the Lord.*13* And he said: Hear ye therefore, O house of David: Is it a small thing for you to be grievous to men, that you are grievous to my God also?*14* Therefore the Lord himself shall give you a sign. Behold a virgin shall conceive, and bear a son, and his name shall be called Emmanuel.

Responsorial Psalm: Psalms 24: 1-2, 3-4ab, 5-6

R. (7c and 10b) Let the Lord enter; he is the king of glory.

1 On the first day of the week, a psalm for David. The earth is the Lord's and the fulness thereof: the world, and all they that dwell therein.

2 For he hath founded it upon the seas; and hath prepared it upon the rivers.

R. Let the Lord enter; he is the king of glory.

3 Who shall ascend into the mountain of the Lord: or who shall stand in his holy place?

4 The innocent in hands, and clean of heart, who hath not taken his soul in vain.

R. Let the Lord enter; he is the king of glory.

5 He shall receive a blessing from the Lord, and mercy from God his Saviour.

6 This is the generation of them that seek him, of them that seek the face of the God of Jacob.

R. Let the Lord enter; he is the king of glory.

Alleluia

R. Alleluia, alleluia.

O Key of David, opening the gates of God's eternal Kingdom: come and free the prisoners of darkness!

R. Alleluia, alleluia.

Gospel: Luke 1: 26-38

26 And in the sixth month, the angel Gabriel was sent from God into a city of Galilee, called Nazareth,*27* To a virgin espoused to a man whose name was Joseph, of the house of David; and the virgin's name was Mary.*28* And the angel being come in, said unto her: Hail, full of grace, the Lord is with thee: blessed art thou among women.*29* Who having heard, was troubled at his saying, and thought with herself what manner of salutation this should be.*30* And the angel said to her: Fear not, Mary, for thou hast found grace with God.*31* Behold thou shalt conceive in thy womb, and shalt bring forth a son; and thou shalt call his name Jesus.*32* He shall be great, and shall be called the Son of the most High; and the Lord God shall give unto him the throne of David his father; and he shall reign in the house of Jacob for ever.*33* And of his kingdom there shall be no end.*34* And Mary said to the angel: How shall this be done, because I know not man?*35* And the angel answering, said to her: The Holy Ghost shall come upon thee, and the power of the most High shall overshadow thee. And therefore also the Holy which shall be born of thee shall be called the Son of God.*36* And behold thy cousin Elizabeth, she also hath conceived a son in her old age; and this is the sixth month with her that is called barren:*37* Because no word shall be impossible with God.*38* And Mary said: Behold the handmaid of the Lord; be it done to me according to thy word. And the angel departed from her.

December 21, 2024

Saturday of the Third Week of Advent

First Reading: Songs 2: 8-14 or Zephaniah 3: 14-18a

8 The voice of my beloved, behold he cometh leaping upon the mountains, skipping over the hills.*9* My beloved is like a roe, or a young hart. Behold he standeth behind our wall, looking through the windows, looking through the lattices.*10* Behold my beloved speaketh to me: Arise, make haste, my love, my dove, my beautiful one, and come.*11* For winter is now past, the rain is over and gone.*12* The flowers have appeared in our land, the time of pruning is come: the voice of the turtle is heard in our land:*13* The fig tree hath put forth her green figs: the vines in flower yield their sweet smell. Arise, my love, my beautiful one, and come:*14* My dove in the clefts of the rock, in the hollow places of the wall, shew me thy face, let thy voice sound in my ears: for thy voice is sweet, and thy face comely.

Or

14 Give praise, O daughter of Sion: shout, O Israel: be glad, and rejoice with all thy heart, O daughter of Jerusalem.*15* The Lord hath taken away thy judgment, he hath turned away thy enemies: the king of Israel the Lord is in the midst of thee, thou shalt fear evil no more.*16* In that day it shall be said to Jerusalem: Fear not: to Sion: Let not thy hands be weakened.*17, 18a* The Lord thy God in the midst of thee is mighty, he will save: he will rejoice over thee with gladness, he will be silent in his love, he will be joyful over thee in praise.

Responsorial Psalm: Psalms 33: 2-3, 11-12, 20-21

R. (1a, 3a) Exult, you just, in the Lord! Sing to him a new song.

2 Give praise to the Lord on the harp; sing to him with the psaltery, the instrument of ten strings.

3 Sing to him a new canticle, sing well unto him with a loud noise.

R. Exult, you just, in the Lord! Sing to him a new song.

11 But the counsel of the Lord standeth for ever: the thoughts of his heart to all generations.

12 Blessed is the nation whose God is the Lord: the people whom he hath chosen for his inheritance.

R. Exult, you just, in the Lord! Sing to him a new song.

20 Our soul waiteth for the Lord: for he is our helper and protector.

21 For in him our heart shall rejoice: and in his holy name we have trusted.

R. Exult, you just, in the Lord! Sing to him a new song.

Alleluia

R. Alleluia, alleluia.

O Emmanuel, our King and Giver of Law: come to save us, Lord our God!

R. Alleluia, alleluia.

Gospel: Luke 1: 39-45

39 And Mary rising up in those days, went into the hill country with haste into a city of Juda.*40* And she entered into the house of Zachary, and saluted Elizabeth.*41* And it came to pass, that when Elizabeth heard the salutation of Mary, the infant leaped in her womb. And Elizabeth was filled with the Holy Ghost:*42* And she cried out with a loud voice, and said: Blessed art thou among women, and blessed is the fruit of thy womb.*43* And whence is this to me, that the mother of my Lord should come to me?*44* For behold as soon as the voice of thy salutation sounded in my ears, the infant in my womb leaped for joy.*45* And blessed art thou that hast believed, because those things shall be accomplished that were spoken to thee by the Lord.

December 22, 2024

Fourth Sunday of Advent

First Reading: Micah 5: 1-4a

1 Now shalt thou be laid waste, O daughter of the robber: they have laid siege against us, with a rod shall they strike the cheek of the judge of Israel.*2* AND THOU, BETHLEHEM Ephrata, art a little one among the thousands of Juda: out of thee shall he come forth unto me that is to be the ruler in Israel: and his going forth is from the beginning, from the days of eternity.*3* Therefore will he give them up even till the time wherein she that travaileth shall bring forth: and the remnant of his brethren shall be converted to the children of Israel.*4* And he shall stand, and feed in the strength of the Lord, in the height of the name of the Lord his God: and they shall be converted, for now shall he be magnified even to the ends of the earth.

Responsorial Psalm: Psalms 80: 2-3, 15-16, 18-19

R. (4) Lord, make us turn to you; let us see your face and we shall be saved.

2 Give ear, O thou that rulest Israel: thou that leadest Joseph like a sheep. Thou that sittest upon the cherubims, shine forth

3 Before Ephraim, Benjamin, and Manasses. Stir up thy might, and come to save us.

R. Lord, make us turn to you; let us see your face and we shall be saved.

15 Turn again, O God of hosts, look down from heaven, and see, and visit this vineyard:

16 And perfect the same which thy right hand hath planted: and upon the son of man whom thou hast confirmed for thyself.

R. Lord, make us turn to you; let us see your face and we shall be saved.

18 Let thy hand be upon the man of thy right hand: and upon the son of man whom thou hast confirmed for thyself.

19 And we depart not from thee, thou shalt quicken us: and we will call upon thy name.

R. Lord, make us turn to you; let us see your face and we shall be saved.

Second Reading: Hebrews 10: 5-10

5 Wherefore when he cometh into the world, he saith: Sacrifice and oblation thou wouldest not: but a body thou hast fitted to me:*6* Holocausts for sin did not please thee.*7* Then said I: Behold I come: in the head of the book it is written of me: that I should do thy will, O God.*8* In saying before, Sacrifices, and oblations, and holocausts for sin thou wouldest not, neither are they pleasing to thee, which are offered according to the law.*9* Then said I: Behold, I come to do thy will, O God: he taketh away the first, that he may establish that which followeth.*10* In the which will, we are sanctified by the oblation of the body of Jesus Christ once.

Alleluia: Luke 1: 38

R. Alleluia, alleluia.

38 Behold, I am the handmaid of the Lord. May it be done to me according to your word.

R. Alleluia, alleluia.

Gospel: Luke 1: 39-45

39 And Mary rising up in those days, went into the hill country with haste into a city of Juda.*40* And she entered into the house of Zachary, and saluted Elizabeth.*41* And it came to pass, that when Elizabeth heard the salutation of Mary, the infant leaped in her womb. And Elizabeth was filled with the Holy Ghost:*42* And she cried out with a loud voice, and said: Blessed art thou among women, and blessed is the fruit of thy womb.*43* And whence is this to me, that the mother of my Lord should come to me?*44* For behold as soon as the voice of thy salutation sounded in my ears, the infant in my womb leaped for joy.*45* And blessed art thou that hast believed, because those things shall be accomplished that were spoken to thee by the Lord.

December 23, 2024

Monday of the Fourth Week of Advent
First Reading: Malachi 3: 1-4, 23-24

1 Behold I send my angel, and he shall prepare the way before my face. And presently the Lord, whom you seek, and the angel of the testament, whom you desire, shall come to his temple. Behold he cometh, saith the Lord of hosts.*2* And who shall be able to think of the day of his coming? and who shall stand to see him? for he is like a refining fire, and like the fuller's herb:*3* And he shall sit refining and cleansing the silver, and he shall purify the sons of Levi, and shall refine them as gold, and as silver, and they shall offer sacrifices to the Lord in justice.*4* And the sacrifice of Juda and of Jerusalem shall please the Lord, as in the days of old, and in the ancient years.*23* Behold I will send you Elias the prophet, before the coming of the great and dreadful day of the Lord.*24* And he shall turn the heart of the fathers to the children, and the heart of the children to their fathers: lest I come, and strike the earth with anathema.

Responsorial Psalm: Psalms 25: 4-5ab, 8-9, 10 and 14

R. (Luke 21:28) Lift up your heads and see; your redemption is near at hand.

4 Let all them be confounded that act unjust things without cause. shew, O Lord, thy ways to me, and teach me thy paths.

5ab Direct me in thy truth, and teach me; for thou art God my Saviour.

R. Lift up your heads and see; your redemption is near at hand.

8 The Lord is sweet and righteous: therefore he will give a law to sinners in the way.

9 He will guide the mild in judgment: he will teach the meek his ways.

R. Lift up your heads and see; your redemption is near at hand.

10 All the ways of the Lord are mercy and truth, to them that seek after his covenant and his testimonies.

14 The Lord is a firmament to them that fear him: and his covenant shall be made manifest to them.

R. Lift up your heads and see; your redemption is near at hand.

Alleluia

R. Alleluia, alleluia.

O King of all nations and keystone of the Church; come and save man, whom you formed from the dust!

R. Alleluia, alleluia.

Gospel: Luke 1: 57-66

57 Now Elizabeth's full time of being delivered was come, and she brought forth a son.58 And her neighbours and kinsfolks heard that the Lord had shewed his great

mercy towards her, and they congratulated with her.*59* And it came to pass, that on the eighth day they came to circumcise the child, and they called him by his father's name Zachary.*60* And his mother answering, said: Not so; but he shall be called John.*61* And they said to her: There is none of thy kindred that is called by this name.*62* And they made signs to his father, how he would have him called.*63* And demanding a writing table, he wrote, saying: John is his name. And they all wondered.*64* And immediately his mouth was opened, and his tongue loosed, and he spoke, blessing God.*65* And fear came upon all their neighbours; and all these things were noised abroad over all the hill country of Judea.*66* And all they that had heard them laid them up in their heart, saying: What an one, think ye, shall this child be? For the hand of the Lord was with him.

December 24, 2024

Tuesday of the Fourth Week of Advent
Mass in the Morning

First Reading: Second Samuel 7: 1-5, 8b-12, 14a, 16

1 And it came to pass when the king sat in his house, and the Lord had given him rest on every side from all his enemies,*2* He said to Nathan the prophet: Dost thou see that I dwell in a house of cedar, and the ark of God is lodged within skins?*3* And Nathan said to the king: Go, do all that is in thy heart: because the Lord is with thee.*4* But it came to pass that night, that the word of the Lord came to Nathan, saying:*5* Go, and say to my servant David: Thus saith the Lord: Shalt thou build me a house to dwell in?*8b* Thus saith the Lord of hosts: I took thee out of the pastures from following the sheep to be ruler over my people Israel:*9* And I have been with thee wheresoever thou hast walked, and have slain all thy enemies from before thy face: and I have made thee a great man, like unto the name of the great ones that are on the earth.*10* And I will appoint a place for my people Israel, and I will plant them, and they shall dwell therein, and shall be disturbed no more: neither shall the children of iniquity afflict them any more as they did before,*11* From the day that I appointed judges over my people Israel: and I will give thee rest from all thy enemies. And the Lord foretelleth to thee, that the Lord will make thee a house.*12* And when thy days shall be fulfilled, and thou shalt sleep with thy fathers, I will raise up thy seed after thee, which shall proceed out of thy bowels, and I will establish his kingdom. *14a* I will be to him a father, and he shall be to me a son. *16* And thy house shall be faithful, and thy kingdom for ever before thy face, and thy throne shall be firm for ever.

Responsorial Psalm: Psalms 89: 2-3, 4-5, 27 and 29

R. (2) For ever I will sing the goodness of the Lord.

2 The mercies of the Lord I will sing for ever. I will shew forth thy truth with my mouth to generation and generation.

3 For thou hast said: Mercy shall be built up for ever in the heavens: thy truth shall be prepared in them.

R. For ever I will sing the goodness of the Lord.

4 I have made a covenant with my elect: I have sworn to David my servant:

5 Thy seed will I settle for ever. And I will build up thy throne unto generation and generation.

R. For ever I will sing the goodness of the Lord.

27 He shall cry out to me: Thou art my father: my God, and the support of my salvation.

29 I will keep my mercy for him for ever: and my covenant faithful to him.

R. For ever I will sing the goodness of the Lord.

Alleluia

R. Alleluia, alleluia.

O Radiant Dawn, splendor of eternal light, sun of justice: come and shine on those who dwell in darkness and in the shadow of death.

R. Alleluia, alleluia.

Gospel: Luke 1: 67-79

67 And Zachary his father was filled with the Holy Ghost; and he prophesied, saying:68 Blessed be the Lord God of Israel; because he hath visited and wrought the redemption of his people:69 And hath raised up an horn of salvation to us, in the house of David his servant:70 As he spoke by the mouth of his holy prophets, who are from the beginning:71 Salvation from our enemies, and from the hand of all that hate us:72 To perform mercy to our fathers, and to remember his holy testament,73 The oath, which he swore to Abraham our father, that he would grant to us,74 That being delivered from the hand of our enemies, we may serve him without fear,75 In holiness and justice before him, all our days.76 And thou, child, shalt be called the prophet of the Highest: for thou shalt go before the face of the Lord to prepare his ways:77 To give knowledge of salvation to his people, unto the remission of their sins:78 Through the bowels of the mercy of our God, in which the Orient from on high hath visited us:79 To enlighten them that sit in darkness, and in the shadow of death: to direct our feet into the way of peace.

December 25, 2024

The Nativity of the Lord (Christmas)
Mass during the Day

First Reading: Isaiah 52: 7-10

7 How beautiful upon the mountains are the feet of him that bringeth good tidings, and that preacheth peace: of him that sheweth forth good, that preacheth salvation, that saith to Sion: Thy God shall reign!8 The voice of thy watchmen: they have lifted up their voice, they shall praise together: for they shall see eye to eye when the Lord shall convert Sion.9 Rejoice, and give praise together, O ye deserts of Jerusalem: for the Lord hath comforted his people: he hath redeemed Jerusalem.10 The Lord hath prepared his holy arm in the sight of all the Gentiles: and all the ends of the earth shall see the salvation of our God.

Responsorial Psalm: Psalms 98: 1, 2-3, 3-4, 5-6

R. (3c) All the ends of the earth have seen the saving power of God.

1 Sing ye to the Lord anew canticle: because he hath done wonderful things. His right hand hath wrought for him salvation, and his arm is holy.

R. All the ends of the earth have seen the saving power of God.

2 The Lord hath made known his salvation: he hath revealed his justice in the sight of the Gentiles.

3ab He hath remembered his mercy his truth toward the house of Israel.

R. All the ends of the earth have seen the saving power of God.

3cd All the ends of the earth have seen the salvation of our God.

4 Sing joyfully to God, all the earth; make melody, rejoice and sing.

R. All the ends of the earth have seen the saving power of God.

5 Sing praise to the Lord on the harp, on the harp, and with the voice of a psalm:

6 With long trumpets, and sound of comet. Make a joyful noise before the Lord our king:

R. All the ends of the earth have seen the saving power of God.

Second Reading: Hebrews 1: 1-6

1 God, who, at sundry times and in divers manners, spoke in times past to the fathers by the prophets, last of all,2 In these days hath spoken to us by his Son, whom he hath appointed heir of all things, by whom also he made the world.3 Who being the brightness of his glory, and the figure of his substance, and upholding all things by the word of his power, making purgation of sins, sitteth on the right hand of the majesty on high.4 Being made so much better than the angels, as he hath inherited a more excellent name than they.5 For to which of the angels hath he said at any time, Thou art my Son, today have I begotten thee? And again, I will be to him a Father, and he shall be to me a Son?6 And again, when he bringeth in the first begotten into the world, he saith: And let all the angels of God adore him.

Alleluia

R. Alleluia, alleluia.

A holy day has dawned upon us. Come, you nations, and adore the Lord. For today a great light has come upon the earth.

R. Alleluia, alleluia.

Gospel: John 1: 1-18

1 In the beginning was the Word, and the Word was with God, and the Word was God.*2* The same was in the beginning with God.*3* All things were made by him: and without him was made nothing that was made.*4* In him was life, and the life was the light of men.*5* And the light shineth in darkness, and the darkness did not comprehend it.*6* There was a man sent from God, whose name was John.*7* This man came for a witness, to give testimony of the light, that all men might believe through him.*8* He was not the light, but was to give testimony of the light.*9* That was the true light, which enlighteneth every man that cometh into this world.*10* He was in the world, and the world was made by him, and the world knew him not.*11* He came unto his own, and his own received him not.*12* But as many as received him, he gave them power to be made the sons of God, to them that believe in his name.*13* Who are born, not of blood, nor of the will of the flesh, nor of the will of man, but of God.*14* And the Word was made flesh, and dwelt among us, (and we saw his glory, the glory as it were of the only begotten of the Father,) full of grace and truth.*15* John beareth witness of him, and crieth out, saying: This was he of whom I spoke: He that shall come after me, is preferred before me: because he was before me.*16* And of his fulness we all have received, and grace for grace.*17* For the law was given by Moses; grace and truth came by Jesus Christ.*18* No man hath seen God at any time: the only begotten Son who is in the bosom of the Father, he hath declared him.

December 26, 2024

Feast of Saint Stephen, first martyr

First Reading: Acts 6: 8-10; 7: 54-59

8 And Stephen, full of grace and fortitude, did great wonders and signs among the people.*9* Now there arose some of that which is called the synagogue of the Libertines, and of the Cyrenians, and of the Alexandrians, and of them that were of Cilicia and Asia, disputing with Stephen.*10* And they were not able to resist the wisdom and the spirit that spoke.

7:54 Now hearing these things, they were cut to the heart, and they gnashed with their teeth at him.*55* But he, being full of the Holy Ghost, looking up steadfastly to heaven, saw the glory of God, and Jesus standing on the right hand of God.*56* And he said: Behold, I see the heavens opened, and the Son of man standing on the right hand of God.*57* And they crying out with a loud voice, stopped their ears, and with one accord ran violently upon him.*58* And casting him forth without the city, they stoned him; and the witnesses laid down their garments at the feet of a young man, whose name was Saul.*59* And they stoned Stephen, invoking, and saying: Lord Jesus, receive my spirit.

Responsorial Psalm: Psalms 31: 3cd-4, 6 and 8ab, 16bc and 17

R. (6) Into your hands, O Lord, I commend my spirit.

3cd Be thou unto me a God, a protector, and a house of refuge, to save me.

4 For thou art my strength and my refuge; and for thy name's sake thou wilt lead me, and nourish me.

R. Into your hands, O Lord, I commend my spirit.

6 Into thy hands I commend my spirit: thou hast redeemed me, O Lord, the God of truth.

8ab I will be glad and rejoice in thy mercy.

R. Into your hands, O Lord, I commend my spirit.

16bc Deliver me out of the hands of my enemies; and from them that persecute me.

17 Make thy face to shine upon thy servant; save me in thy mercy.

R. Into your hands, O Lord, I commend my spirit.

Alleluia: Psalms 118: 26a, 27a

R. Alleluia, alleluia.

26a, 27a Blessed is he who comes in the name of the LORD: the LORD is God and has given us light.

R. Alleluia, alleluia.

Gospel: Matthew 10: 17-22

17 But beware of men. For they will deliver you up in councils, and they will scourge you in their synagogues.*18* And you shall be brought before governors, and before kings for my sake, for a testimony to them and to the Gentiles:*19* But when they shall deliver you up, take no thought how or what to speak: for it shall be given you in that hour what to speak.*20* For it is not you that speak, but the Spirit of your Father that speaketh in you.*21* The brother also shall deliver up the brother to death, and the father the son: and the children shall rise up against their parents, and shall put them to death.*22* And you shall be hated by all men for my name's sake: but he that shall persevere unto the end, he shall be saved.

December 27, 2024

Feast of Saint John, Apostle and evangelist

First Reading: First John 1: 1-4

1 That which was from the beginning, which we have heard, which we have seen with our eyes, which we have looked upon, and our hands have handled, of the word of life:*2* For the life was manifested; and we have seen and do bear witness, and declare unto you the life eternal, which was with the Father, and hath appeared to us:*3* That which we have seen and have heard, we declare unto you, that you also may have fellowship with us, and our fellowship may be with the Father, and with his Son Jesus Christ.*4* And these things we write to you, that you may rejoice, and your joy may be full.

Responsorial Psalm: Psalms 97: 1-2, 5-6, 11-12

R. (12) Rejoice in the Lord, you just!

1 The Lord hath reigned, let the earth rejoice: let many islands be glad.

2 Clouds and darkness are round about him: justice and judgment are the establishment of his throne.

R. Rejoice in the Lord, you just!

5 The mountains melted like wax, at the presence of the Lord: at the presence of the Lord of all the earth.

6 The heavens declared his justice: and all people saw his glory.

R. Rejoice in the Lord, you just!

11 Light is risen to the just, and joy to the right of heart.

12 Rejoice, ye just, in the Lord: and give praise to the remembrance of his holiness.

R. Rejoice in the Lord, you just!

Alleluia: See Te Deum

R. Alleluia, alleluia.

We praise you, O God, we acclaim you as Lord; the glorious company of Apostles praise you.

R. Alleluia, alleluia.

Gospel: John 20: 1a and 2-8

1a And on the first day of the week,*2* Mary Magdalen ran, therefore, and cometh to Simon Peter, and to the other disciple whom Jesus loved, and saith to them: They have taken away the Lord out of the sepulchre, and we know not where they have laid him.*3* Peter therefore went out, and that other disciple, and they came to the sepulchre.*4* And they both ran together, and that other disciple did outrun Peter, and came first to the sepulchre.*5* And when he stooped down, he saw the linen cloths lying; but yet he went not in.*6* Then cometh Simon Peter, following him, and went into the sepulchre, and saw the linen cloths lying,*7* And the napkin that had been about his head, not lying with the linen cloths, but apart, wrapped up into one place.*8* Then that other disciple also went in, who came first to the sepulchre: and he saw, and believed.

December 28, 2024

Feast of the Holy Innocents, martyrs

First Reading: First John 1: 5 – 2: 2

5 And this is the declaration which we have heard from him, and declare unto you: That God is light, and in him there is no darkness.*6* If we say that we have fellowship with him, and walk in darkness, we lie, and do not the truth.*7* But if we walk in the light, as he also is in the light, we have fellowship one with another, and the blood of Jesus Christ his Son cleanseth us from all sin.*8* If we say that we have no sin, we deceive ourselves, and the truth is not in us.*9* If we confess our sins, he is faithful and just, to forgive us our sins, and to cleanse us from all iniquity.*10* If we say that we have not sinned, we make him a liar, and his word is not in us.*2:1* My little children, these things I write to you, that you may not sin. But if any man sin, we have an advocate with the Father, Jesus Christ the just:*2* And he is the propitiation for our sins: and not for ours only, but also for those of the whole world.

Responsorial Psalm: Psalms 124: 2-3, 4-5, 7b-8

R. (7) Our soul has been rescued like a bird from the fowler's snare.

2 If it had not been that the Lord was with us, When men rose up against us,

3 Perhaps they had swallowed us up alive. When their fury was enkindled against us,

R. Our soul has been rescued like a bird from the fowler's snare.

4 Perhaps the waters had swallowed us up.

5 Our soul hath passed through a torrent: perhaps our soul had passed through a water insupportable.

R. Our soul has been rescued like a bird from the fowler's snare.

7b The snare is broken, and we are delivered.

8 Our help is in the name of the Lord, who made heaven and earth.

R. Our soul has been rescued like a bird from the fowler's snare.

Alleluia: See Te Deum

R. Alleluia, alleluia.

We praise you, O God, we acclaim you as Lord; the white-robed army of martyrs praise you.

R. Alleluia, alleluia.

Gospel: Matthew 2: 13-18

13 And after they were departed, behold an angel of the Lord appeared in sleep to Joseph, saying: Arise, and take the child and his mother, and fly into Egypt: and be there until I shall tell thee. For it will come to pass that Herod will seek the child to destroy him.*14* Who arose, and took the child and his mother by night, and retired into Egypt: and he was there until the death of Herod:*15* That it might be fulfilled which the Lord spoke by the prophet, saying: Out of Egypt have I called my son.*16* Then Herod perceiving that he was deluded by the wise men, was exceeding angry; and sending killed all the men children that were in Bethlehem, and in all the borders thereof, from two years old and under, according to the time which he had diligently inquired of the wise men.*17* Then was fulfilled that which was spoken by Jeremias the prophet, saying:*18* A voice in Rama was heard, lamentation and great mourning; Rachel bewailing her children, and would not be comforted, because they are not.

December 29, 2024

Feast of the Holy Family of Jesus, Mary and Joseph

First Reading: First Samuel 1: 20-22, 24-28 or Sirach 3: 2-6, 12-14

20 And it came to pass when the time was come about, Anna conceived and bore a son, and called his name Samuel: because she had asked him of the Lord.*21* And Elcana her husband went up, and all his house, to offer to the Lord the solemn sacrifice, and his vow.*22* But Anna went not up: for she said to her husband: I will not go till the child be weaned, and till I may carry him, that he may appear before the Lord, and may abide always there.*24* And after she had weaned him, she carried him with her, with three calves, and three bushels of flour, and a bottle of wine, and she brought him to the house of the Lord in Silo. Now the child was as yet very young:*25* And they immolated a calf, and offered the child to Heli.*26* And Anna said: I beseech thee, my lord, as thy soul liveth, my lord: I am that woman who stood before thee here praying to the Lord.*27* For this child did I pray, and the Lord hath granted me my petition, which I asked of him.*28* Therefore I also have lent him to the Lord all the days of his life, he shall be lent to the Lord. And they adored the Lord there. And Anna prayed, and said:

Or

2 For God hath made the father honourable to the children: and seeking the judgment of the mothers, hath confirmed it upon the children.*3* He that loveth God, shall obtain pardon for his sins by prayer, and shall refrain himself from them, and shall be heard in the prayer of days.*4* And he that honoureth his mother is as one that layeth up a treasure.*5* He that honoureth his father shall have joy in his own children, and in the day of his prayer he shall be heard.*6* He that honoureth his father shall enjoy a long life: and he that obeyeth the father, shall be a comfort to his mother.*12* Son, support the old age of thy father, and grieve him not in his life;*13* And if his understanding fail, have patience with him, and despise him not when thou art in thy strength: for the relieving of the father shall not be forgotten.*14* For good shall be repaid to thee for the sin of thy mother.

Responsorial Psalm: Psalms 84: 2-3, 5-6, 9-10 or Psalms 128: 1-2, 3, 4-5

R. (5a) Blessed are they who dwell in your house, O Lord.

2 How lovely are thy tabernacles, O Lord of host!

3 My soul longeth and fainteth for the courts of the Lord. My heart and my flesh have rejoiced in the living God.

R. Blessed are they who dwell in your house, O Lord.

5 Blessed are they that dwell in thy house, O Lord: they shall praise thee for ever and ever.

6 Blessed is the man whose help is from thee: in his heart he hath disposed to ascend by steps,

R. Blessed are they who dwell in your house, O Lord.

9 O Lord God of hosts, hear my prayer: give ear, O God of Jacob.

10 Behold, O God our protector: and look on the face of thy Christ.

R. Blessed are they who dwell in your house, O Lord.

Or

R. (1) Blessed are those who fear the Lord and walk in his ways.

1 Blessed are all they that fear the Lord: that walk in his ways.

2 For thou shalt eat the labours of thy hands: blessed art thou, and it shall be well with thee.

R. Blessed are those who fear the Lord and walk in his ways.

3 Thy wife as a fruitful vine, on the sides of thy house.

R. Blessed are those who fear the Lord and walk in his ways.

4 Behold, thus shall the man be blessed that feareth the Lord.

5 May the Lord bless thee out of Sion: and mayest thou see the good things of Jerusalem all the days of thy life.

R. Blessed are those who fear the Lord and walk in his ways.

Second Reading: First John 3: 1-2, 21-24 or Colossians 3: 12-21

1 Behold what manner of charity the Father hath bestowed upon us, that we should be called, and should be the sons of God. Therefore the world knoweth not us, because it knew not him.*2* Dearly beloved, we are now the sons of God; and it hath not yet appeared what we shall be. We know, that, when he shall appear, we shall be like to him: because we shall see him as he is.*21* Dearly beloved, if our heart do not reprehend us, we have confidence towards God:*22* And whatsoever we shall ask, we shall receive of him: because we keep his commandments, and do those things which are pleasing in his sight.*23* And this is his commandment, that we should believe in the name of his Son Jesus Christ: and love one another, as he hath given commandment unto us.*24* And he that keepeth his commandments, abideth in him, and he in him. And in this we know that he abideth in us, by the Spirit which he hath given us.

Or

12 Put ye on therefore, as the elect of God, holy, and beloved, the bowels of mercy, benignity, humility, modesty, patience:*13* Bearing with one another, and forgiving one another, if any have a complaint against another: even as the Lord hath forgiven you, so do you also.*14* But above all these things have charity, which is the bond of perfection:*15* And let the peace of Christ rejoice in your hearts, wherein also you are called in one body: and be ye thankful.*16* Let the word of Christ dwell in you abundantly, in all wisdom: teaching and admonishing one another in psalms, hymns, and spiritual canticles, singing in grace in your hearts to God.*17* All whatsoever you do in word or in work, do all in the name of the Lord Jesus Christ, giving thanks to God and the Father by him.*18* Wives, be subject to your husbands, as it behoveth in the Lord.*19* Husbands, love your wives, and be not bitter towards them.*20* Children, obey your parents in all things: for this is well pleasing to the Lord.*21* Fathers, provoke not your children to indignation, lest they be discouraged.

Alleluia: Colossians 3: 15a, 16a or Acts 16: 14b

R. Alleluia, alleluia.

15a, 16a Let the peace of Christ control your hearts; Let the word of Christ dwell in you richly.

R. Alleluia, alleluia.

Or

R. Alleluia, alleluia.

14b Open our hearts, O Lord, to listen to the words of your Son.

R. Alleluia, alleluia.

Gospel: Luke 2: 41-52

41 And his parents went every year to Jerusalem, at the solemn day of the pasch,*42* And when he was twelve years old, they going up into Jerusalem, according to the custom of the feast,*43* And having fulfilled the days, when they returned, the child Jesus remained in Jerusalem; and his parents knew it not.*44* And thinking that he was in the company, they came a day's journey, and sought him among their kinsfolks and acquaintance.*45* And not finding him, they returned into Jerusalem, seeking him.*46* And it came to pass, that, after three days, they found him in the temple, sitting in the midst of the doctors, hearing them, and asking them questions.*47* And all that heard him were astonished at his wisdom and his answers.*48* And seeing him, they wondered. And his mother said to him: Son, why hast thou done so to us? behold thy father and I have sought thee sorrowing.*49* And he said to them: How is it that you sought me? did you not know, that I must be about my father's business?*50* And they understood not the word that he spoke unto them.*51* And he went down with them, and came to Nazareth, and was subject to them. And his mother kept all these words in her heart.*52* And Jesus advanced in wisdom, and age, and grace with God and men.

December 30, 2024

The Sixth Day in the Octave of Christmas

First Reading: First John 2: 12-17

12 I write unto you, little children, because your sins are forgiven you for his name's sake.*13* I write unto you, fathers, because you have known him, who is from the beginning. I write unto you, young men, because you have overcome the wicked one.*14* I write unto you, babes, because you have known the Father. I write unto you, young men, because you are strong, and the word of God abideth in you, and you have overcome the wicked one.*15* Love not the world, nor the things which are in the world. If any man love the world, the charity of the Father is not in him.*16* For all that is in the world, is the concupiscence of the flesh, and the concupiscence of the eyes, and the pride of life, which is not of the Father, but is of the world.*17* And the world passeth away, and the concupiscence thereof: but he that doth the will of God, abideth for ever.

Responsorial Psalm: Psalms 96: 7-8a, 8b-9, 10

R. (11a) Let the heavens be glad and the earth rejoice!

7 Bring ye to the Lord, O ye kindreds of the Gentiles, bring ye to the Lord glory and honour:

8a Bring to the Lord glory unto his name.

R. Let the heavens be glad and the earth rejoice!

8b Bring up sacrifices, and come into his courts:

9 Adore ye the Lord in his holy court. Let all the earth be moved at his presence.

R. Let the heavens be glad and the earth rejoice!

10 Say ye among the Gentiles, the Lord hath reigned. For he hath corrected the world, which shall not be moved: he will judge the people with justice.

R. Let the heavens be glad and the earth rejoice!

Alleluia

R. Alleluia, alleluia.

A holy day has dawned upon us. Come, you nations, and adore the Lord. Today a great light has come upon the earth.

R. Alleluia, alleluia.

Gospel: Luke 2: 36-40

36 And there was one Anna, a prophetess, the daughter of Phanuel, of the tribe of Aser; she was far advanced in years, and had lived with her husband seven years from her virginity.*37* And she was a widow until fourscore and four years; who departed not from the temple, by fastings and prayers serving night and day.*38* Now she, at the same hour, coming in, confessed to the Lord; and spoke of him to all that looked for the redemption of Israel.*39* And after they had performed all things according to the law of the Lord, they returned into Galilee, to their city Nazareth.*40* And the child grew, and waxed strong, full of wisdom; and the grace of God was in him.

December 31, 2024

The Seventh Day in the Octave of Christmas

First Reading: First John 2: 18-21

18 Little children, it is the last hour; and as you have heard that Antichrist cometh, even now there are become many Antichrists: whereby we know that it is the last hour.*19* They went out from us, but they were not of us. For if they had been of us, they would no doubt have remained with us; but that they may be manifest, that they are not all of us.*20* But you have the unction from the Holy One, and know all things.*21* I have not written to you as to them that know not the truth, but as to them that know it: and that no lie is of the truth.

Responsorial Psalm: Psalms 96: 1-2, 11-12, 13

R. (11a) Let the heavens be glad and the earth rejoice!

1 Sing ye to the Lord a new canticle: sing to the Lord, all the earth.

2 Sing ye to the Lord and bless his name: shew forth his salvation from day to day.

R. Let the heavens be glad and the earth rejoice!

11 Let the heavens rejoice, and let the earth be glad, let the sea be moved, and the fulness thereof:

12 The fields and all things that are in them shall be joyful. Then shall all the trees of the woods rejoice

R. Let the heavens be glad and the earth rejoice!

13 Before the face of the Lord, because he cometh: because he cometh to judge the earth. He shall judge the world with justice, and the people with his truth.

R. Let the heavens be glad and the earth rejoice!

Alleluia: John 1: 14a, 12a

R. Alleluia, alleluia.

14a, 12a The Word of God became flesh and dwelt among us. To those who accepted him he gave power to become the children of God.

R. Alleluia, alleluia.

Gospel: John 1: 1-18

1 In the beginning was the Word, and the Word was with God, and the Word was God.*2* The same was in the beginning with God.*3* All things were made by him: and without him was made nothing that was made.*4* In him was life, and the life was the light of men.*5* And the light shineth in darkness, and the darkness did not comprehend it.*6* There was a man sent from God, whose name was John.*7* This man came for a witness, to give testimony of the light, that all men might believe through him.*8* He was not the light, but was to give testimony of the light.*9* That was the true light, which enlighteneth every man that cometh into this world.*10* He was in the world, and the world was made by him, and the world knew him not.*11* He came unto his own, and his own received him not.*12* But as many as received him, he gave them power to be made the sons of God, to them that believe in his name.*13* Who are born, not of blood, nor of the will of the flesh, nor of the will of man, but of God.*14* And the Word was made flesh, and dwelt among us, (and we saw his glory, the glory as it were of the only begotten of the Father,) full of grace and truth.*15* John beareth witness of him, and crieth out, saying: This was he of whom I spoke: He that shall come after me, is preferred before me: because he was before me.*16* And of his fulness we all have received, and grace for grace.*17* For the law was given by Moses; grace and truth came by Jesus Christ.*18* No man hath seen God at any time: the only begotten Son who is in the bosom of the Father, he hath declared him.

Made in the USA
Las Vegas, NV
14 September 2024